# Explored

Elwyn Gruffudd

Gwasg Carreg Gwalch

First published in 2018

Map: Alison Davies, Mapping Co Ltd



ISBN: 978-1-84524-277-0
Cover design: Eleri Owen

Published by Gwasg Carreg Gwalch,
12 Iard yr Orsaf, Llanrwst, Wales LL26 0EH
tel: 01492 642031
email: books@carreg-gwalch.cymru
website: www.carreg-gwalch.cymru

*Conwy quay, castle and estuary*

# Contents

# Introduction

The Conwy river flows northwards along the eastern flank of the Snowdonia mountains. The valley is a geological border between the high peaks and glacial cwms to the west and the hilly farmland to the east. It is also a historical border between the strongholds of the Welsh kings in the mountains and invading armies from the east – Romans, Saxons and Normans have periodically occupied parts of the valley banks over the ages.

Two main towns lie near its often contested estuary. Conwy is one of the most historic towns in Wales and has been an important port on the western side of the estuary. Llandudno has also very old roots, but the main town that we view today was built as a resort in Victorian times.

## The historic town of Conwy

On a few occasions, the memory of a town and its locality will linger for a lifetime – and Conwy is such a town. First impressions are often misleading and a newcomer to the shores of the Conwy estuary will easily be forgiven for believing

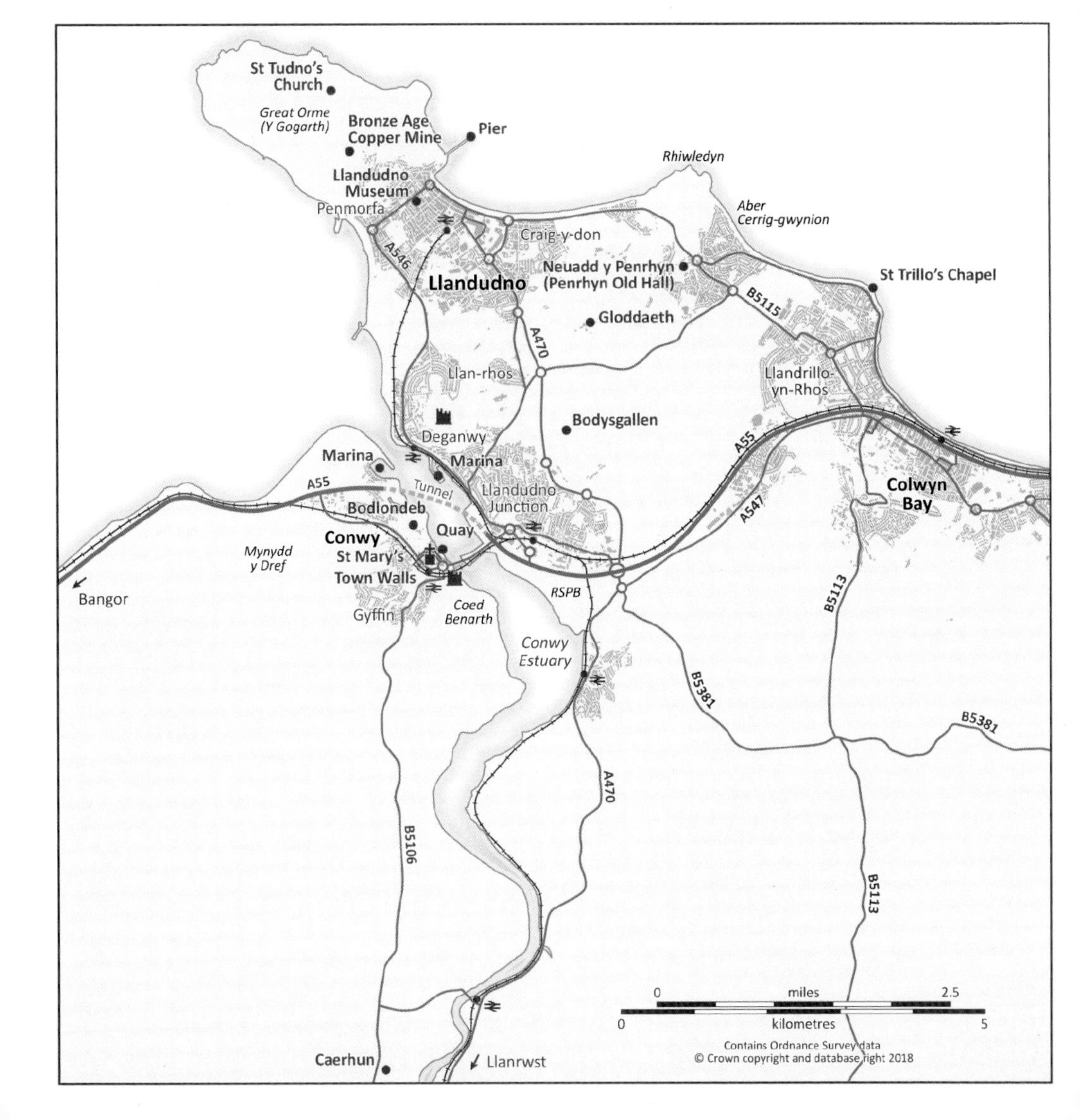
St Tudno's Church
Great Orme (Y Gogarth)
Bronze Age Copper Mine
Pier
Rhiwledyn
Llandudno Museum
Penmorfa
Aber Cerrig-gwynion
Craig-y-don
A546
Neuadd y Penrhyn (Penrhyn Old Hall)
Llandudno
St Trillo's Chapel
B5115
Gloddaeth
A470
Llan-rhos
Llandrillo-yn-Rhos
Bodysgallen
Deganwy
A55
Marina
Marina
Tunnel
Llandudno Junction
Colwyn Bay
A55
Bodlondeb
A547
Conwy
Quay
Mynydd y Dref
St Mary's
Town Walls
Bangor
RSPB
B5113
Gyffin
Coed Benarth
Conwy Estuary
B5381
B5381
A470
B5106
B5113
0
miles
2.5
0
kilometres
5
Contains Ordnance Survey data
© Crown copyright and database right 2018
Caerhun
Llanrwst

that Conwy town story begins and ends with the building of its castle and its well-preserved town walls.

It is certainly a majestic castle, but Conwy's tidal waters had been a haven and a frontier for centuries before its short military service to the Norman kings. The quay quickly grew to be mightier than its towering fortress and the former colony evolved to be a significant market town and a river port servicing the Welsh heartland that at one time it was meant to tame.

Today, the colours of history are alive on the estuary waters, the narrow, renovated streets, the historic houses – there are over 200 listed buildings within its walls – and the lively quayside. The past was built in layers and a wealth of depth is felt under the skin of present-day Conwy.

**Llandudno: *'Hardd, Hafan, Hedd'* – A beautiful haven of peace**

Llandudno is Wales' favourite seaside resort. Visitors are attracted by Llandudno's superb setting and unique heritage. Holidaymakers love the town's sophisticated hotels, restaurants and cafes and local people from miles around come to Llandudno to shop and be entertained.

Best known as a beautiful nineteenth century bathing place, the locality has a much older history. Y Gogarth (*Great Orme*), the larger of the two limestone headlands that define Llandudno Bay, looms over the town inviting visitors to explore its ancient landscape. At the opposite end of the bay a cave on the Little Orme was long ago the scene of the secret printing of the first Welsh book printed in Wales.

Llandudno's mild climate and limestone headlands provide a unique natural environment for many special animals and plants. So if you're out exploring on the Great Orme keep an eye open for the beautiful silver-studded blue butterfly and Llandudno's famous wild Kashmir goats.

The Queen of Romania visited in 1890 and bequeathed to the town a description so apt it continues to serve as Llandudno's official motto: "*Hardd, Hafan, Hedd*".

*1. The bay from the Great Orme;*
*2. The prom at Llandudno*

1

2

# The Ancient Landscape of the Great Orme

Limestone is the key to Llandudno's unique environment and history. The town's beautiful horseshoe-shaped bay is defined by twin limestone headlands (Great Orme and Little Orme). Llandudno's oldest buildings are composed of limestone and many of the area's rarest plants depend on underlying limestone to supply essential nutrients.

Llandudno's characteristic limestone was formed over three hundred million years ago under a warm tropical sea. Ancient fossilised life-forms can be easily identified in the exposed rocks of Bishop's quarry on Great Orme. Llandudno's shimmering, limestone promontories attracted the first tourists 13,000 years ago when a party of Stone Age hunter-gatherers rested in a cave above the present Empire Hotel. Other Stone Age remains have been found in caves at Pant y wennol, Tan-y-bryn and the Little Orme, where the skeleton of Blodwen, the town's first named resident was discovered in 1890.

We don't know much about how these ancient people lived but they've left us intriguing reminders of their deaths. In a field on Great Orme stands a cromlech that served as a collective burial place, another can be found on a rocky shelf at Nant-y-gamar.

Adept at shaping stones into useful tools, these early Llandudno residents must have been perplexed as they frequently uncovered bits of shiny green coloured rock. Such stones appeared useless for tool making and were discarded until someone noticed that the green rocks surrounding the camp fire seemed to change with the effects of the heat. Or perhaps the secret of the stones was brought by an ancient traveller. In any case, four thousand years ago, the beauty and utility hidden within Llandudno's copper-bearing limestone was tapped for the first time. Soon Great Orme resounded to the digging and scraping of ancient metal mining. By adding a small

*1. The coastal road under the limestone cliffs; 2. Orme cave dwellers as recreated at Llandudno Museum; 3. The Gogarth cromlech*

BONE TOOLS
Over 30,000 bones have been
found during the last 13 years
of excavation, they derive
ainly from:- Cattle, Sheep,

amount of tin to their molten copper the ancient metalsmiths found they could produce even more enduring tools and the Bronze Age began. Llandudno became a very important place. Archaeologists believe it was probably the only copper mine in Britain being worked full time, a hub of the Bronze Age industrial revolution. But the process involved more than mere technology for turning rock into shiny metal made bronze-smiths into magicians and Llandudno into a sacred place, blessed by the gods as a repository of magical metal.

New materials stimulated new ideas and new ceremonies. Life in Llandudno was changing, people were no longer buried in communal graves but cremated and their remains put in vases or *cistiau* before being covered over with gleaming stones. A Bronze Age burial cairn remains on Great Orme although three other sites were destroyed in the nineteenth century when the Marine Drive, Augusta Street and Madog Street were laid out. Fortunately the magnificent surviving remains of two Bronze Age round houses at Coed-gaer provide us with impressive consolation.

*1. Bronze Age copper mine on the Orme;*
*2. Bone tools of the early miners;*
*3. One of the underground finds;*
*4. Limestone pavement near the Orme's summit*

# Lost Lands and New Worlds

Myths sometimes hold truths that are lost in historical facts and scientific studies. Near Conwy, earlier inhabitants lived in Brythonic villages, Celtic hillforts, Bronze Age settlements and prehistoric caves. Over the centuries, they shared a common heritage which was handed down in an oral tradition in their Celtic/Brythonic language. This was later filtered through into the inheritance of the Welsh descendants of these earlier people, and today the Welsh language holds the key to a very old culture.

An important part of that culture was literature – epic legends and well-crafted poetry. Nearly always, these were based on old tribal memories and are signposts to pieces of lost histories. Welsh medieval literature in the princes' courts of Gwynedd (the province of north-western Wales), re-echoed the tales that were told around the fires of circular Celtic hut-dwellers on Mynydd y Dref, behind Conwy, and even in the prehistoric caves of Y Gogarth – called the *Great Orme* by the Vikings, as it resembled a sea serpent from their longships.

Scientific research certifies that old tree stumps revealed at the lowest tides on sandy banks between Penmaenmawr and Llandudno are the remains of a submerged forest, 7,000 years old. Out there also are boulders aligned at regular angles: a formation called 'Llys Helig'. Geological deposits? Old weirs?

Legend has it that this was once the fine court of Helig ap Glannawg, lord of the lowlands. His daughter's lover murdered a young nobleman for the want of his golden torc. He then heard whispers '*Dial a ddaw, dial a ddaw*' ('revenge will come, revenge will come'). Four generations later, during singing and dancing in a great feast at Llys Helig, a maid discovered fish swimming in the cellar when she went for more wine. The sea dykes had broken and by the following morning, a bay of seawater covered all the lush lands of Helig and his court lied submerged forever – apart from those brief moments at low tide, which

*The Celtic hillfort remains at Mynydd y Dref, Conwy*

were enough to keep the legend alive through the ages (see Michael Senior's *Llys Helig and the myth of lost lands*).

Historians, generally, agree that sea-adventurers from Japan or Europe visited the American continent long before Columbus. Madog was the youngest son of Owain Gwynedd, a twelfth century ruler of northern Wales. He preferred the sea to the mountain rocks, and learned seafaring skills from fishermen and merchants. Tired of war on the mainland, he sailed westwards, where the Celts always believed lied the Land of the Forever Young. He set sail from the mouth of Afon Ganol, beyond Deganwy hills to the east of Aberconwy. After many years, his ship reappeared over the horizon. He and his followers had found a great new land in the west and he appealed for volunteers to settle there. He then captained a fleet of ten ships and sailed for America for the last time.

Footholds yielded, new opportunities gained – these myths hold the essence of Conwy's history.

# Celtic Settlers and Roman Legionaries

Pendinas, an ancient hillfort on Great Orme still dominates modern Llandudno. A pathway leads you up and through fallen ramparts to wander freely amongst the remains of almost a hundred Iron Age huts. Imagine the tales told in those thatched, Celtic roundhouses around the fire by members of the tribe that farmed Great Orme. The Celtic Iron Age was an era with a reverence for the land, for the sea, for the stars and above all for the oral tradition. The Celts preserved and enlivened their histories through stories, songs and above all, poetry – and that rich heritage lives on in modern-day Welsh literature and culture.

Farming had become tougher since Bronze Age times. The climate had deteriorated and there was competition for good land. Tribes had constructed fortified enclosures, like Pendinas, so that families and their animals could retire behind defensible boundaries if threatened by rival tribes or invaders.

The Celts were fierce in defence but creative, cultured and artistic. Their decorative metalwork is legendary and a superb example, resembling a horse brass, was discovered on the slopes of Little Orme in the 1990s. The awkward, elevated location of the find suggests that, like so much of the Celtic metalware that has been discovered, it was probably intended to be a votive offering, a gift to the gods.

Reverence for nature was fundamental to Celtic tradition with springs, wells and water especially revered. Valuable items were often cast into the water to appease the spirit of the well. Llandudno preserves several ancient wells and amongst the most intriguing are Ffynnon Sadwrn, Craigside and Ffynnon Rufeinig on Great Orme. Does the first date back to the time of Sadwrn, the brother of the Celtic saint, Illtud? Perhaps it refers to the Roman god Saturn or maybe it just reminds us that it was the locally-favoured well for drawing the water for brewing Saturday's beer?

The derivation of Ffynnon Rufeinig (Roman well) seems clearer, most people

*An old quarry and an enclosure wall on the Orme's summit*

1

2

3

think it was the well used by the Romans for washing copper ore mined on Great Orme. Although archaeologists have found thousands of Bronze Age stone hammers in the mines they have yet to discover any metal Roman tools. Ffynnon Rufeinig may well be an ancient well but the name first appeared in Victorian times and was probably chosen to appeal to English visitors.

Celtic society continued in this area, influenced but not destroyed by the nearby legions of Rome. The language and culture of the area evolved and developed under Roman occupation, but Celtic peoples speaking the Welsh language greeted travellers who brought Christianity in the sixth century 'Age of the Saints'.

1, 2, 3, *Pendinas Celtic hillfort;*
4. *The Roman well*

# Roman Eagles and Welsh Dragons

Slowly, the Romans pioneered a road along the northern coast of Wales and crossed the Conwy river about 3 miles (4.8 km) upriver of Conwy town. Here they built a fort to guard the ford and the port: Caerhun.

Other Roman interest in the area were the copper mines on the Great Orme above Llandudno, where they further exploited prehistoric works, and the pearl mussels of the river bed. They claimed that Conwy pearls were the largest and most beautiful throughout the British Isles. Occasional pearls have been found in the Conwy down the centuries – the last one in 1953.

The Romans left these lands at the mercy of foreign hordes but a strong leader, Cunedda, defended Welsh shores against attacks. From him, the ancestry of the royal line of Wales may be traced. In that line stands Maelgwn Gwynedd (died 549) who had his seat of power on the two hills above Deganwy, on the eastern bank of the Conwy estuary. He fought and won a famous battle on the sandy dunes of Morfa Rhiannedd, where the streets of Llandudno were laid down thirteen centuries later. After the death of King Arthur in 546, Maelgwn was elected the king of the Welsh to carry on the resistance against the Anglians and Saxons and was known as 'the Dragon of the Island'.

He was also strong in cunning. He claimed superiority on other chieftains in northern Wales following a canute-style contest at Aberdyfi. Each rival brought his throne to the water's edge and whoever held out longest against the incoming tide would be declared an overlord. The other proud leaders brought their ceremonial thrones, decorated with heavy metals and stones. Maelgwn brought a simple seat of goose-quills and wax and as he floated above the rest, so was the hierarchy of the kings of Deganwy secured.

Tradition has it that Maelgwn surrounded himself with poets and in his court was held the earliest record of a Welsh Eisteddfod (a cultural event where

*1. Caerhun church on the site of the Roman fort; 2. The path to Deganwy castle site; 3. The twin hills of Deganwy*

1

2

3

1

2

poets, musicians and singers display their talents and compete). Under the king's patronage, a congress of bards and musicians was held at Deganwy castle. Maelgwn decided that a competition between the two crafts was to be held on Mynydd y Dref, above Conwy. Any boats had been previously hid and all the competitors had to swim across the Conwy river before the contest. As a result, the harps and pipes were useless and the poets – favoured by Maelgwn, of course – carried the day.

One of Maelgwn's poets prophecised that the Welsh would 'praise their lord, keep their language and lose all their lands – except the wild terrain of Wales'. During the king's lifetime, Saxon and Germanic tribes had already established themselves in eastern Britain. Vikings would soon be on the horizon. But Maelgwn had established a dynasty that would secure the safety of Gwynedd which would set an example and vision that would occasionally unify the whole of Wales to stand against invaders.

*1. Stone remains at Deganwy;*
*2. The castle's view of the estuary;*
*3. Conwy marina from Deganwy*

# The Llan of Saint Tudno

Llandudno is named after a Celtic missionary who, in the sixth century, sailed to Great Orme from his home in southern Wales. Sheltering in a cave he so impressed people with the simplicity and sincerity of his faith that they helped him erect a crude wooden shelter to serve as a meeting place. The enclosed area around such a holy place was known as a *llan*, and the site on Great Orme was Tudno's *llan* or Llandudno.

The Christianity brought by Tudno, and spread throughout the Celtic countries of Ireland, Cornwall, Isle of Man, Scotland, Wales and Brittany, was earlier and very different from the religion brought from Rome by Saint Augustine on the orders of Pope Gregory. Celtic Christianity was rooted in the old ways, with a reverence for nature, for simplicity and for monasticism. When, in 693, Saint Augustine demanded obedience from the Welsh bishops he was firmly rebuffed. The long-established Church in Wales owed nothing to Imperial Rome and was determined to resist domination.

Tudno's original building was rebuilt in stone in the twelfth century but has retained its simplicity and its setting.

Another Celtic saint, Trillo, began his mission a little further east of Llandudno at a place now known as Llandrillo-yn-Rhos. Trillo's cell was later also rebuilt in stone and has even more perfectly preserved its original Celtic simplicity. There is only enough room inside Trillo's tiny seafront church to accommodate six worshippers and the covered well that originally supplied the saint's water supply can be seen in front of the altar. The preservation of the well and its position at the very heart of the church provides powerful testimony to the enduring reverence for ancient wells that leads us back through Celtic Christianity to our pagan Iron Age Celtic ancestors.

Perhaps that enduring Celtic spirit of closeness to nature and love of simplicity led Welsh Christians in a later era to be so critical of what the Established Anglican

*The winding road up the Great Orme to St Tudno's church*

Church had become by the eighteenth century. Llandudno's numerous chapels remind us that it wasn't just in ancient times that Welsh Christians maintained their distinct traditions.

Amongst the most impressive of Llandudno's marvellous chapels is Tabernacl in Upper Mostyn Street. The Baptists were the first of Llandudno's non-conformists to gain much success. They began preaching in the yard of a public house, Yr Hen Dafarn, on the slopes of Great Orme in 1789. Converts to the Baptist cause were baptised in the sea at Penmorfa (West Shore). By 1813 they had sufficient members to erect Tabernacl chapel, which was later rebuilt and extended to cope with an ever-increasing membership.

In the twentieth century Tabernacl hit the headlines when its minister, the Reverend Lewis Valentine was imprisoned for setting fire to an Air Ministry bombing school as a political protest. On his release he was welcomed back to Tabernacl and hailed as a Welsh hero.

4

5

*1. St Tudno's church; 2. Inside St Tudno's; 3. St Trillo's chapel; 4. Reverend Lewis Valentine's chapel and memorial plaque*

# The Court of Maelgwn Gwynedd

Just south of Llandudno stand the ruins of Deganwy castle. Dominating the twin hills overlooking the Conwy river the view is magnificent and the position of huge strategic importance. Dominance of the Conwy estuary was essential to prevent invaders from gaining control of the lush farmlands of Dyffryn Conwy and access into the mountains of Snowdonia.

In the sixth century this hilltop was fortified and Deganwy castle created by Maelgwn Gwynedd, who was not only the most powerful king in Wales but on the death of Arthur in 546AD the man elected 'King of all the Brythoniaid'. His kingdom included all the territories in southern Scotland, England, Wales and Cornwall which were resisting the invasion of their island. Maelgwn was a warrior with a fiercesome reputation whose task was to keep at bay the Saxon and Germanic hordes who were determined to exploit the withdrawal of the Roman legions from Britain.

In his youth Maelgwn might have been a Celtic monk but once he turned to pursue the martial path to kingship he drew the wrath of Gildas, the renowned chronicler of the age. Gildas denounced Maelgwn's struggle for power and accused him of murdering his own wife and nephew. Yet Gildas acknowledged Maelgwn's success as a military and political leader and called him, *Insularis Draco*, Dragon or High-King of the Island.

Maelgwn ruled supreme, the kingdom of Gwynedd was known and feared throughout the land. Cunning, cultured but with a continuing love for Celtic Christianity Maelgwn is said to have founded the church at Llanrhos for his private devotions and the hill overlooking the church, Bryn Maelgwn, still bears his name. The ancient well near the church provides further evidence of its Celtic foundation. In 549AD, inside this very church Maelgwn Gwynedd met his fate. Whilst looking out through the keyhole of the church door at a world increasingly ravaged by the pestilence of the yellow plague his eye beheld a terrible sight. At

*Llandudno from Deganwy*

the same moment the monstrous creature spreading the disease espied Maelgwn and instantly struck him down. His last resting place is disputed, perhaps he lies buried in the adjacent graveyard or maybe he was carried to the top of Bryn Maelgwn but historians agree that after Maelgwn's death it was many years before Wales could again feel so peaceful and secure.

*1. The Great Orme from Mynydd y Dref, Conwy; 2. Celtic hillfort on the mountain; 3. The view down towards the estuary*

# A Deganwy Stronghold

For centuries, the story of Conwy's estuary was the history of Wales. It was contested but not conquered; snatched but never surrendered. Vikings attacked from the western sea; Anglians and Saxons from the east and the wooden fort of Deganwy was destroyed by lightning in 810.

But an able leader was found in Rhodri, who guarded his shores with a fleet of warships. The Vikings were to kill all the royal families of England – bar Wessex – and occupy expansive territories there, but were denied a foothold in Wales. Rhodri defeated the Vikings in 856, killing Horm their king, and gained an international reputation. He united the whole of Wales as one nation and became known as Rhodri Mawr – the first in Welsh history to carry the title 'the Great'.

He was killed in battle in 878, but his sons carried on with his work, defeating the Anglians of Mercia for the last time in a battle at Cymryd near Conwy three years later. It became known to the Welsh as '*Dial Rhodri*', Rhodri's revenge.

A new invader extended his shadow across the Conwy river after 1066. The Norman earl, Robert of Rhuddlan, built a new stone castle at Deganwy around 1080 but again Gwynedd rose – under Gruffudd ap Cynan this time – who landed three ships at Deganwy and Robert was cut down by Welsh spears in the battle which followed.

The Normans were driven by the same greed and power that had already seen the whole of England succumb in a few months. The Anglo-Saxons leaders were decimated forever, the serfs became second-class citizens. Theirs was not the language of law or government.

Wales, in the same period, saw a burst of military and literary activity. Poets sang in Welsh for their princes, recording their deeds, indicating also that there was a national renaissance and a new political awareness. Gruffudd's son, Owain, extended the territory of Gwynedd to the English border, consolidating his gains by building castles. Henry II assembled a great army at Oswestry in 1165 and attacked Wales, but was met by an united

Welsh force from every corner of Wales. Foul weather and hard terrain demoralized Henry's army. He retreated, burning churches, mutilating hostages. Seeds of further bitterness were sown.

Fathers passed on bows and spears to sons and often the guerilla tactics of the Welsh grinded down armies that outnumbered them. Foreign mercenaries hardly dared to cross the Conwy river and challenge the mountain fortress of Snowdonia, and for centuries, the river was a natural moat keeping the enemy at bay.

Deganwy, however, was on the eastern side of the river and exchanged hands many times during the conflict as armies approached along the strip of lowland along the coast of north-eastern Wales. The Welsh kept their distances at times, resisted fiercely when the opportunity came, kept the river as a final line of defence and survived.

*An old ford crosses the Conwy at Cymryd – the site of the 'Dial Rhodri' battle*

# Voyages of Destruction and Discovery

After the death of Maelgwn Gwynedd, Wales was increasingly isolated from other Celtic Britons as the Saxons grew ever more dominant. The Welsh language emerged quite distinct from the old Brythonic form once spoken from Cornwall to central Scotland. Sharing a distinct language nourished feelings of common identity, of belonging to Wales.

Llandudno's geographical position left it exposed to seaborne raids. From the ninth to the eleventh centuries Vikings menaced the coast.

These *Black Pagan* raiders sought slaves and precious metals and evidence of a Viking attack on Llandudno was uncovered on Great Orme in 1980. Four silver coins, minted in Viking Dublin in 1025 and probably dropped during the course of a raid, were discovered near Saint Tudno's church. But the Vikings

*Aber Cerrig-gwynion, looking towards Llandrillo-yn-Rhos*

couldn't rape and pillage at will. When Rhodri Mawr united the three kingdoms of Powys, Deheubarth and Gwynedd in the ninth century, Llandudno was strong enough to resist. There is a possibility that Rhodri's victory is commemorated in the name 'Great Orme'; others maintain that 'Orme' is Norse for 'sea serpent'.

Yet even Rhodri's contribution to Llandudno's maritime heritage is dwarfed by the twelfth century efforts of Madog ab Owain Gwynedd. A commemorative plaque erected at Fort Morgan, on the coast of Alabama by the Daughters of the American Revolution summarises his achievement, '*In memory of Prince Madog, a Welsh explorer who landed on the shores of Mobile Bay in 1170 and left behind, with the Indians, the Welsh language*'.

According to Welsh tradition Madog reached America more than 300 years before Columbus but was so sympathetically received by the natives that the Mandan Indians adopted the Welsh language for themselves. Madog began this epic voyage of discovery from a small harbour at Penrhyn Bay. The original dock has been built over and a sea wall erected but its position at the head of Afon Ganol is marked by a large bungalow named Odstone, which retains fragments of the original harbour in its front garden. Affixed to the ancient stonework is a tablet bearing the legend that, *Prince Madog sailed from here, Aber Kerrick-Gwynan 1170AD and landed at Mobile, Alabama, with his ships, Gorn Gwynant and Pedr Sant.*

When studied in detail in the eighteenth century, the Mandan language was discovered to consist of many words resembling Welsh equivalents. A Welshman named Stedman shipwrecked in the 1660s claimed he was rescued by Indians whose language he understood. They told him that their ancestors came from a country named Gwynedd in the isle of Britain. He provided no proof but Professor Gwyn Williams was told by Ronald Little Owl, the last native Mandan speaker, that: 'The lone man was the founder of our people. He was a white man who brought our people in his big canoe across a great water.'

# Tales of Invasion and Liberation

After the Normans conquered England incursions plagued the Conwy estuary. Deganwy castle was captured by the Norman Robert of Rhuddlan in 1080 but attacked and burnt by Llywelyn ap Iorwerth in 1200. In 1210 the Earl of Chester regained and rebuilt the castle but was besieged by Llywelyn and starved into submission before retreating back to England.

Undeterred the Earl raised a bigger, better-equipped army and invaded northern Wales. Faced with disaster the disunited Welsh leadership rallied to Llywelyn's flag and dramatically reversed the fortunes of the Norman-English. Deganwy castle was retaken in 1214 and for many years his kingdom enjoyed peace and prosperity. He was honoured with the title Llywelyn Fawr (*the Great*) but after his death in 1240 English attacks resumed.

In 1245 the English recaptured Deganwy and held onto it until 1263 when it was destroyed by Llywelyn ap Gruffudd (Llywelyn Fawr's grandson). Other Welsh leaders enthusiastically embraced Llywelyn's cause and acclaimed him not just the prince of Gwynedd but Prince of Wales. The King of England demanded that Llywelyn formally submit to him as his feudal overlord but the Welsh jealously guarded their own rights and independence. On 12 November 1276, Llywelyn was chillingly declared a *rebel and disturber of the peace* by Edward I, one of the most greedy tyrants that ever sat on England's throne.

Edward advanced to Deganwy and forced Llywelyn to submit. For six years an uneasy truce reigned until, spurred on by Dafydd, his brother, Llywelyn determined to cast off the English yoke, but during a skirmish in 1282 he was fatally wounded.

Aberconwy abbey was the mausoleum of the princes of Gwynedd and it was where they kept their regalias and treasures. These included the Crown of King Arthur and *Y Groes Nawdd* – a sacred relic used in crowning and homage ceremonies in Wales. These potent

*Llywelyn Fawr's statue at the town square, Conwy*

1
2
3

symbols of Welsh independence were looted by Edward I in 1283 and removed to London, exactly as he stole the Stone of Scone from Scotland in 1296.

Llandudno became the prize of the English Crown who granted the Manor of Gogarth to Bishop Anian of Bangor as a reward for traitorous co-operation. Adding insult to injury at Caernarfon in 1284, Anian proclaimed Edward's son, 'Prince of Wales'. Anian enhanced his Llandudno landholding with the erection of a substantial manor house, known as the Bishop's Palace. Edward directed that produce from the Llandudno area could only be traded through Conwy market, which was taxed and controlled by the colonial power.

In 1400 the flames of freedom were ignited by Owain Glyndŵr. Declared by his comrades as the rightful Prince of Wales he soon controlled the countryside from Anglesey to Glamorgan. Those most hated symbols of English domination – the planted towns and colonial castles – were prime targets of his campaign. In 1401 Glyndŵr's supporters captured Conwy castle and sacked the Bishop's Palace. Faced with suppressing a struggle for national liberation and a possible alliance between France, Scotland and Wales, Henry IV fought back with a vengeance. Glyndŵr's campaign went into reverse and in 1409 his last stronghold fell to English siege-machines. In 1415 Owain Glyndŵr disappeared from history but not from legend. Tradition claims Glyndŵr is sleeping: one day he will awake and lead Wales to independence and freedom.

*1. St Mary's church, Conwy; 2. Tŵr Llywelyn – the site of Llywelyn's great hall; 3. Llywelyn's stone coffin, now at Gwydir Chapel, St Grwst's church, Llanrwst*

# The Abbey of Aberconwy

Greatness in a king is traditionally extended by later generations – it is not a contemporary title handed out by a desire to please a ruling monarch. After Rhodri and Owain, a third great leader hailed from Conwy shores – Llywelyn Fawr (Llywelyn the Great).

His statue stands in the old market square of Conwy today, carrying his full name, Llywelyn ap Iorwerth. On 24 July 1186 he gave a charter to Cistercian monks to establish an abbey – which stood at the site of Conwy's parish church today. He also gave them sea-weir, wrecking and ferry rights, land on the Great Orme and mountain pastures.

Llywelyn also erected a hall (its remains are part of the town walls today) as a royal palace for himself at Aberconwy, as the abbey was called. Llywelyn, after unifying and securing Wales with many famous victories over the Normans, spent his last years within the abbey walls. When he died in 1240, he was interred in front of the high altar. When Edward I evicted the monks from their privileged lands to

*A stone figure found at Deganwy castle – believed to be a carving of one of the two Llywelyn princes*

Maenan to make room for his colonial town, the faithful men took Llywelyn's stone coffin with them. After the Dissolution, it was removed again and now reposes, minus lid and occupant, in Capel Gwydir, Llanrwst parish church.

The abbey was not destined for a quiet, peaceful life however. Twice, King John of England, invaded the district, burning the cathedral at Bangor, but spared Aberconwy abbey. In 1245, Henry III and his army were trapped on the eastern side of the river. Greedy for plunder, 300 rowed across the river, pursued the Welsh and spoiled the abbey of Aberconwy, burning the books and other treasures belonging to it. It robbed Wales of a wealth of archives, literature and historical information.

The abbey became the mausoleum of princes – Gruffudd and Dafydd, Llywelyn Fawr's sons were also laid to rest here. But war was always at its doorstep. Prince Edward of England garrisoned Deganwy castle and another Llywelyn, the grandson of Llywelyn Fawr, besieged it and reduced them to eating the flesh of their own horses and dogs in 1263. Edward surrendered, Deganwy was destroyed forever and in the following treaty Llywelyn ap Gruffudd was confirmed as the prince of the whole of Wales.

But Edward was ruthless and ambitious. His treachery was described by a contemporary English writer by the words: 'When he is cornered he promises whatever you wish but as soon as he is free he forgets his promise.' For a whole year, Edward prepared in detail and at a great cost three huge armies to invade Wales. He forced Llywelyn back to Snowdonia and a treaty was signed in Aberconwy in 1277, stripping the Welsh ruler of most of his lands. Another Welsh War of Independence followed, but Llywelyn was killed by a stray soldier on the banks of Irfon in central Wales. Llywelyn's head was carried on a spear through the streets of London.

Edward's army crossed the Conwy river and in January 1283 captured the Welsh stronghold of Dolwyddelan in the heart of Snowdonia.

# A Castle for a King

Conwy is dominated by its castle. Today, old and ruined, it has an elegant beauty above changing tides and against a backdrop of mountain scenery. Every year, thousands of fascinated visitors walk through its gateway and climb its towers.

There is no doubt that it was a building feat in its day. Edward I arrived in Conwy in March 1283 and within four days of his arrival, arrangements were made to work on new fortifications on the western side of the Conwy river, securing a foothold on Snowdonia's shore. Master engineers, an army of craftsmen and labourers and the services of James of St George, the greatest military architect of the age, were all enlisted in the building of a castle and a walled town that took only four and a half years to complete.

It was a part of a Plantagenet fortresses scheme in northern Wales built to symbolise Norman dominance and subdue the Welsh. It was the largest, most expensive construction programme in medieval Europe. More than 1,500 workers – mostly drawn from all over England – were employed at Conwy alone.

The castle itself is pinned on a rock above the river, and defended by three walls on its western side. The eight drum towers are massive in their strength – it is a compact, great mass of solid masonry created to defend a king's ambition.

A charter was granted to the town on 8 September 1284 and special favours were extended to encourage English settlers. The Welsh were banned from buying land or a house or from holding any office in the town and were only let in for the weekly market, to buy and sell goods at English prices. The aim was to depossess the Welsh of their lands, their commerce, their resources, language and heritage.

The castle's elaborate defences however, betray the weakness of Edward I's position – nowhere else in his territories was such protection called for. Its strategy was to defend a foothold rather than to conquer the whole of Snowdonia. Originally, it was whitewashed to catch the sunlight and draw attention to its standards, there, within reach of the dark mountains. No doubt it also attracted the

*Only a Norman foothold on Welsh land: Conwy castle*

glare of any Welsh people who would view it from the distance.

On more than one occasion, the invaders were extremely grateful for its physical sturdiness. In 1294-5, Madog ap Llywelyn of royal Welsh blood, led a revolt against the castle towns, burning Caernarfon and besieging Conwy. Edward was trapped in his own masonry in its castle, cut off from his army and his provisions. Here the proud king was obliged to live on water and a little honey until the danger passed.

In the end, these castles are stone skeletons which testify to hollow victories and are, by today, sources of pride in their own resilience to the Welsh people who are now responsible for their upkeep. A restoration programme was started in 1953 and by 1987 the castle and the town walls of Conwy – together with Beaumaris, Caernarfon and Harlech – are inscribed on the World Heritage List as a historic site of outstanding universal value.

*The Welsh stronghold in the hinterland is an ever-present backdrop to the castle*

# A Town Behind Walls

Conwy town maintained its medieval harp-shape for centuries – it did not outgrow its town walls until twentieth century estates were built at Gyffin and on Sychnant road. It still constitutes one of the best-preserved castle and walled towns in Europe.

It was, like other fortress towns in northern Wales, a garrisoned island which could be comfortably supplied from the sea. For centuries, the Welsh countryside was considered too dangerous for any infiltration by government officials or even armed forces that were not exceptionally strong in numbers. Wales outside the walled towns lived a life of its own, but behind the strong stonework Welsh laws and customs were prohibited. A free borough was granted to the burgesses of Conwy and adventurers and speculators from England and France were invited to settle here. Trading and racial rights were thrown at them. As local historian Christopher Draper puts it: 'The castle and walled town were the chosen device for producing and enforcing a new, loyal, ethnically-cleansed settlement' (*Walks from Conwy*).

The privileged, fortified township was challenged by generations of Welsh uprisings. After Madog's revolt of 1294-5, the Welsh awaited for Owain Lawgoch – a Welsh prince in exile who fought as a French captain against the English. His 1372 fleet, sailing for Wales, was hampered by bad weather and an English assassination terminated his life in Montagne-sur-Gironde in 1378.

In 1400, the charismatic Owain Glyndŵr led a revolt which saw every foreign castle and town in Wales attacked as he laid down the foundations of modern Wales with his vision of an independent government, church and university. In the spring of 1401, Gwilym and Rhys ap Tudur, Anglesey noblemen, brothers in arms and forefathers of Henry Tudor of Wales, besieged Conwy's walls. On Good Friday, while the garrison soldiers were in church, the gateway had been wedged open by a rebel sympathiser and the Welshmen captured the castle without shedding a drop of blood and burnt the town and its mill. The unthinkable had happened! An English army marched on the town and

SAFLE BWS
BUS STOP

attacked the castle, but all in vain. Finally, when their provisions ran low the Welsh left the town through negotiation, surrendering nine hostages to the English. They left and Glyndŵr's campaign went from strength to strength, but the nine hostages were promptly executed.

Conwy again saw action and its garrison was thoroughly demoralised during the long years of Owain Glyndŵr's campaign. The valley was wasted during the War of the Roses when the Earl of Pembroke led a great army through Snowdonia and then a temporary peace followed. The influence of the fortress receded and the old alien family names died out. Early records are full of Hookes, Robinsons, Burches and Porters but by Tudor times, Welsh families were established within Conwy's town walls. The colony had passed away; Conwy from then onwards is a Welsh town.

# Tŷ Aberconwy and other old buildings

One of the best known houses in Conwy is Tŷ Aberconwy, standing on one of the original plots that lined Castle Street and High Street, now a National Trust property. It is traditionally dated at 1400 and might have survived the destruction of Glyndŵr's uprising; on the other hand it was possibly built from the ashes after the Tudur brothers put the town to the torch in 1401. Either way it is the best surviving example of a medieval town house in northern Wales.

It was once the home of a successful merchant and the ground floor was used as a bakery and a fish and chip shop, among other things. Today, it has been restored to its past glory, with a National Trust shop in the basement and the upper two floors housing an audio-visual presentation showing the daily life of Conwy through different periods of its history, with furnished rooms displaying traditional Welsh furniture on loan from St Fagans National Museum of History.

Originally, Conwy was a town of a few streets and many gardens and was well-known for its herbs, flowers, fruits and honey. Two of Conwy's traditional fairs continue to be held to this day, Ffair Hadau (seed fair) on 26 March and Ffair Fêl (honey fair) on 13 September. The name of Berry Street, leading northwards from Tŷ Aberconwy however is misleading – it was originally Burial Street where the dead of the 1607 plague were buried in the street. Workmen were to find bones here when digging up the road at a later date and a large number of skeletons were revealed when part of High Street was lowered and repaired.

Further up Castle Street from Tŷ Aberconwy is the striking building, the old Black Lion – a vicarage at one time, it still displays a memorial stone with the inscription '1589 I.B.E.'. It was built in that year for Vicar John Bricknall (I being the Latin form of J) and his wife Em. Later it became a tavern, a coaching inn and an antique shop. Every Monday morning a pig market used to be held there. On Castle Street also is the much-altered Old

*Tŷ Aberconwy*

HIGH ST

Olde College
D. Wyn Roberts Ltd
CHILDREN'S
WEAR

College building (now a menswear shop). It is said to have its foundations in the old abbey of Aberconwy and was later extensively remodelled, but fragments of it could be the oldest parish stone walls in the town.

The beautiful parish church of St Mary is the oldest building in the town, incorporating the remains of the abbey in the west wall of its tower, including three lancet windows. As the town prospered in the later Middle Ages, the church enjoyed its share of good fortune. The great eastern window was erected in the chancel, the font was built in Tudor times and the tower was raised. Its rood screen is particularly impressive – it used to accommodate singers and musicians as well as a small organ.

The churchyard also includes many interesting features – a sundial, the 'we are seven' grave of Wordsworth fame as well as seats for a tranquil moment to take in the beauty and the historic connections.

*1. The parish church in the centre of the town;*
*2. The Old College;*
*3. The Black Lion; 4. St Mary's bell tower*

# The Welsh Gentry of Plas Mawr

Plas Mawr was built between 1576 and 1585 for Robert Wynn – a Welshman and a member of the Wynn family that had already established itself on an estate around its home at Castell Gwydir, Llanrwst. The family had already gained power and land by careful politics during the early Tudor era, and acquired the property of Aberconwy abbey (then at Maenan) at the Crown's dissolution of the monasteries. Robert Wynn was a remarkable and well-travelled trader and belonged to the class of Welsh gentry who gave precedence to personal profits before Welsh patriotism during the Elizabethan era. He had, however, an European flair and many features of Plas Mawr display his continental connections.

Plas Mawr is noted for its ornamental plasterwork, many of it embellished by various crests, shields and arms of the old kings and princes of Wales, as the Wynns traced their ancestry back to early royal bloodlines with pride. The three eagles of Owain Gwynedd are seen here, the 'three severed Englishman's heads' of Ednyfed Fychan, Grand Forester of Snowdonia; the *fleur-de-lys* of Collwyn ap Tango, lord of Eifionydd and Ardudwy and the red dragon of King Cadwaladr and Henry VII. It is rich in ornamentation, the finest surviving town house of the Elizabethan era to be found anywhere in Britain. It was authentically renovated at the end of the twentieth century, which included restoring and repainting the original plasterwork and lime-rendering the outside walls.

The beauty of the building today is the effect of the blend in its design of the traditional halls of the local Welsh gentry and the Renaissance-style features that Robert Wynn encountered on his European travels. In many ways, Plas Mawr would not look out of place in the historic towns of Flanders or the Netherlands, but the oak beams and slate roofing give it a distinct Welsh flavour. Robert Wynn died in 1598 and was buried in the parish church, after a good life in

*Plas Mawr, Conwy*

R
15
80

oriel
gallery
EXHIBITION

Conwy 'where he kept worthy plentiful house all his time'.

Plas Mawr was the home of the Royal Cambrian Academy from 1886 until recently – it is now housed in the former Congregational Chapel nearby. The RCA promoted artists in Victorian Conwy and was established at a meeting in a Llandudno Junction hotel in 1881.

Turning left into Chapel Street from Crown Lane, which runs alongside Plas Mawr, a vacant plot with stone memorials is reached. Here stood another fine medieval house, Parlwr Mawr, where John Williams was born in 1582. He became Archbishop of York in 1641 and was a strong supporter of the crown during the Civil War. He repaired the castle and garrisoned the town at his own expense. During the conflict however, he switched sides after his loyalty was not reciprocated by King Charles, and assisted Parliamentary forces in gaining control of the town. Parlwr Mawr survived until 1948 when it was demolished for safety reasons when no public body accepted responsibility for its restoration.

# Cave Printers of Rhiwledyn

In Tudor times Roman Catholics were often treated as disloyal, as potential agents of foreign powers, of Spain or the Pope. Queen Elizabeth controlled church practice and was determined to prevent the new technology of printing being used to promote the Catholic faith.

Many people in Wales privately wished to see a return to the Catholic faith but the Pugh family of Penrhyn Old Hall were prepared to openly defy the Crown. In 1582 their adherence to the Old Faith earned them a 'Writ of Outlawry', served by the High Sheriff of Caernarfon. Robert Pugh did not recant but instead determined to establish a secret printing press to publish Catholic literature. He decided that a cave on Rhiwledyn – a part of the Little Orme, not far from Penrhyn Hall would provide a suitably secret yet not too inconvenient venue for his illicit venture.

Sometime in the 1580s Pugh guided small boats carrying the printing equipment, inks, cases of lead type and paper into a cove adjacent to his chosen cave. After assembling the press Robert was joined in his enterprise by Father William Davies, a priest born in Colwyn Bay but trained at Rheims. Davies brought with him from France the manuscript of *Y Drych Cristnogawl* (The Christian Mirror).

From autumn 1586 until spring 1587 William Davies and Robert Pugh, ably assisted by other members of the family, printed off copies of the small format, 180-page book. They may well also have received skilled help from an English printer called Roger Thackwell who was known amongst his contemporaries as, 'Knave Thackwell . . . which printed popish and traitorous Welsh books in Wales'.

In April 1587 a shepherd on Little Orme spotted smoke rising from the cave and went to investigate. He passed details of what he saw to the local magistrate, Sir Thomas Mostyn. Now Mostyn was caught between a rock and a hard place, he had no alternative but to carry out his

*1. Penrhyn Old Hall;*
*2. Eastern cliffs of Rhiwledyn*

responsibility as an agent of the Crown yet he had no wish to condemn to possible death the family of his near neighbour and fellow gentryman Robert Pugh.

Mostyn assembled a large force to arrest the lawbreakers but on reaching the cave at dusk fell, he decided it would be wiser to post a guard and wait until morning before attempting a thorough search. Providentially this provided an excellent opportunity for the printing party to slip away by a seaward route.

The papist escaped and although the Pughs were eventually pardoned and permitted to return to Penrhyn Hall, William Davies was less fortunate. Apprehended in Beaumaris in 1592 he was hanged, drawn and quartered. Declared a martyr by the Catholic Church, he was beatified by the Pope on 22 November 1987 and a Llandudno primary school was named in his memory.

Local historians continue to debate which of Little Orme's caves housed the papist printers but it is universally acknowledged that the very first Welsh book printed on Welsh soil was published on this quiet eastern edge of Llandudno.

# Mansions of the Gentry

The mild climate and attractively wooded meadows of this area provided an ideal setting for the country houses of the rising gentry class of post medieval Wales. Traditionally the Welsh gentry had been clan leaders with a duty to promote and preserve the interests of kith and kin. As Wales lost its independence the gentry began to shift their loyalties away from serving their own people to serving the English Crown. The crunch came in 1536 when the Act of Union incorporated and subordinated Wales to the Kingdom of England. The Welsh gentry abandoned all pretence of leading their countrymen from English thraldom and embraced the English establishment with embarrassing enthusiasm.

Carrots were dangled before the gentry and like donkeys they dashed for a taste. The primary lure was appointment as a Justice of the Peace. Sixteenth century J.P.'s were powerful instruments of State power and before the century ended the Pughs at Penrhyn, the Mostyns at Gloddaeth and the Wynns of Bodysgallen all secured appointments.

The gentry knew their value to the English establishment lay in being able to deliver to the Crown the loyalty of their fellow countrymen so it was important not to immediately abandon all appearance of Welshness. The Mostyns continued to pay lip service to the bardic tradition whilst denying any wider clan responsibility.

Llandudno's main gentry houses of Gloddaeth, Bodysgallen and Penrhyn Old Hall, all survive though none remains a family home. Gloddaeth was for 500 years the local seat of the Mostyns, Llandudno's most powerful family. They acquired the estate through marriage in 1460 although the oldest part of the existing building dates from 1584. The celebrated prelate and reviled politician, Archbishop John Williams died at Gloddaeth in 1650 and the building is now occupied by St David's College.

Bodysgallen is said by some to have originally been built by Caswallon, a fifth century King of Gwynedd hence Bod Caswallon (Home of Caswallon), but

*Bodysgallen*

others prefer the more prosaic derivation of a place of thistles, *ysgallen*. Whatever its origins, Bodysgallen is full of interest and includes an unusual central lookout tower, a formal seventeenth century Dutch garden and an eighteenth century rose garden. As an up-market hotel and restaurant it allows access to patrons.

The most accessible of Llandudno's old gentry houses is Penrhyn Old Hall which serves as an historic public house and restaurant. It has lost most of its original estate land that once included much of Penrhyn Bay, but it has nevertheless retained much of its Elizabethan character. The origins of Penrhyn Old Hall may well stretch back much further for John Leyland, who visited in 1549, described it as an 'ancient stonehouse'.

1. & 2. *Gloddaeth;*
3. 4. & 5. *Bodysgallen*

# Copper Miners and Crofters

For two thousand years Llandudno's copper mines lay abandoned. The medieval Mines Royal Act made all mining of metals a felony and only after it was repealed in 1688 did copper mining on Great Orme resume. In 1695 the Welsh Copper Company took out a lease on the Llandudno mines. With interruptions for accidents, flooding and market conditions, mining continued for almost two centuries. Before the advent of tourism, mining formed the backbone of Llandudno's economy. In the mines' heyday, from 1830 to 1850, two to three hundred men were directly employed whilst many more, from carters to candle makers, were indirectly dependent on the mines for their income.

Three copper mines operated on Great Orme. The Old Mine developed on the Bishop of Bangor's land, close to the summit; the New Mine worked the land around Pyllau Farm whilst the Tŷ Gwyn operated on the Happy Valley side of the mountain. The miners entered down long wooden ladders or descended stemples, which were rungs set into vertical shafts.

Victorian copper miners discovered tools discarded by ancient predecessors; stag horns, deer bones and stone hammers but assumed the Romans were responsible. Superstitions and myths were rife amongst old miners. Strange noises underground were thought to be the sound of 'knockers', mysterious beings who inhabited the mines. When a lode was worked out it was traditional to leave a token gift for them at the end of the abandoned adit.

Women and children were engaged for surface work by the mine companies. Their usual task was to smash the ore into fragments for smelting and these were loaded on ships bound for Swansea. As the smelting process required far greater quantities of fuel than ore, it made sense to carry out processing near the coalfields of southern Wales.

With no smelting works Llandudno developed no metal finishing or

*Mining exhibitions at the Great Orme Bronze Age Mine and Llandudno Museum*

it was in1987
MALACHITE
(Copper Carbonate)
This was the Copper ore
favoured by Bronze Age miners.

manufacturing trades and so the town never became industrial. There were a few steam-powered pumping engines to prevent flooding of the mines but not much other machinery. When mining was at its most frenzied Llandudno remained rural, even the miners worked the land. Some ran smallholdings but most kept a vegetable plot, a few sheep, a pig or cow and it was common to see thirty or forty miners helping farmers bring in the harvest.

The miners of Great Orme were never reduced to mere wage slaves. When the sun shone they abandoned minework and returned home to attend to gardens, livestock and friends. When John Taylor, an English mining engineer, took control of the Old Mine in 1853 he felt frustrated beyond measure: 'So contrary was this system to any known in any copper mine in Great Britain, or in any mine whatever where we are concerned, either as partners or as managers, that we decided at once to take a stand against it, and to insist upon a full eight hours work per diem which is customary in all well-regulated mines throughout the United Kingdom.'

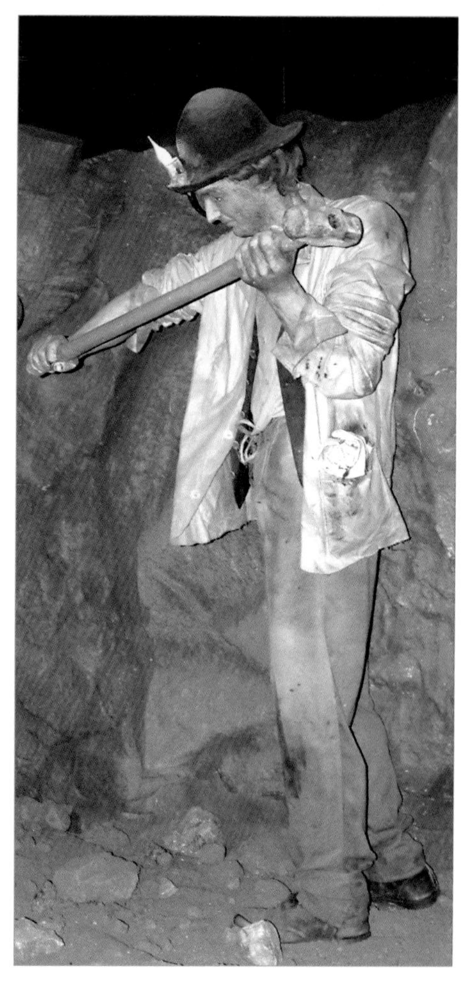

# A River Port

The monks of Aberconwy abbey were granted ferry rights on the estuary by the princes of Gwynedd; the kings of England later demanded these for their own exchequer and for centuries it was the only way to cross the river. Since the days when Conwy was an isolated English outpost, navigation ensured that a lifeline supply of military assistance and essential goods was always within reach. The quay was paramount to the existence of the town, and in peaceful times it grew as a sea harbour for inland goods. In Tudor times, an unusual number of Conwy town houses were roofed with slate – but that is not surprising on realising that slate, and later lead and zinc, were shipped downstream in small boats from Trefriw quay, before being loaded on larger vessels. This continued into the early part of the twentieth century.

The Conwy valley is rich in oak trees. Between 1754 and 1760 alone, £50,000

*The Telford suspension bridge* *The quay at Conwy*

RWAY

worth of best oak was floated down from the Gwydir estate for the shipwrights. Sloops and schooners were built for the coastal trade, carrying copper from Gogarth mines to Swansea bringing coal on the return journey. Potatoes and corn were exported to Liverpool; wheat to Ireland and oatmeal to Scotland and bark for the tanning industry.

The Liverpool Arms on Conwy quay was a favourite haunt of Conwy mariners. In the 1830s, the landlord was a certain Captain Jones who also ran a steamer, the *Conwy Castle*, backwards and forwards between the quay and Liverpool. It covered the 45-mile (72.5 km) trip in five hours and also took foot passengers – five shillings down below or half a crown up on the deck.

When Telford improved the road communications and built an embankment to reach the rocky island from which he suspended his famous bridge, it caused silting upriver. Llansanffraid Glan Conwy lost its significance as a river port but allowed

*The quay at Conwy*

*Deganwy paddle steamer*

1
QUEEN VICTORIA
SIGHTSEEING CRUISES
2
MARINA
3

Conwy to thrive on the lost trade. Conwy's wooden quay was rebuilt by four stonemasons in 1831 and their efforts still stand the floods and the tides under the town walls to this day. Conwy's shipping fortunes was soon to be diminished by the arrival of the railway however, which reached the town in 1849.

Pleasure-seekers provided trade for a different kind of boat however. In their heyday, elegant paddle steamers ferried travellers from Conwy and Deganwy to Trefriw. The service lasted from 1847 to 1940 and it took an hour and a half to make the journey up the tidal river, carrying up to 170 passengers. The tall black funnels of the steamers had special hinges to allow them to fold down to pass beneath the Conwy Suspension Bridge. The trips were finally ceased when warplanes used the Conwy valley for their return flights after bombing Liverpool – river traffic was thought too risky under the circumstances. Smaller paddles continued in the 1950s and today boats still run river cruises from Conwy quay.

*1. & 2. Conwy river cruises;*
*3. Deganwy marina*

# Salmon and Mussels

Conwy fish has been feasted on with relish since time immemorial. An old Irish manuscript relates how St Bridget landed near Deganwy castle after an adventurous crossing from Ireland. According to local legend, she found the people here starving after seasons of bad weather. She threw a handful of reeds into the estuary which immediately turned into long, green-like fish which were fed to the population. The saint, called Ffraid in Welsh, established her chapel at Llansanffraid Glan Conwy, and the migratory fish – *brwyniad* ('reed fish' or sparling/smelt) is still fished with two boats and a seine net on the Conwy river in late March and early April.

Another legend tells of a mermaid who was stranded on a large stone in the estuary. She asked a group of fishermen to save her and throw her back into the sea. They laughed at her plight, but when the tide finally turned and freed her she cursed them as she swam back to the sea. When losses at sea have befallen Conwy, some still think back to the mermaid's words.

Salmon used to be caught in the river also, in the abbey weirs on the eastern side using the old Welsh method – netting with coracles. These had a framework of laths covered with canvas, tightly stretched and coated with pitch to make them watertight. They are very light vessels, easily carried on the back of one man and are still used on three rivers in southern Wales. Salmon netting is still allowed in the estuary but only a few licences remain, inherited from one generation to another within the fishing families of Conwy.

Deep-sea fishermen still bring back catches of plaice and cod to Conwy quay, but the town is probably more famous for its mussels than any other seafood. The gathering of the edible blue mussel, goes back as an industry to the 1840s – again the fast railway connections with the populated towns was a key factor. At one time the shells supported forty full-time fishermen.

The mussels are found in abundance in sandbeds on the bar at the mouth of the river and were gathered daily by men, women and children at ebb-tide. The

*1. Conwy fishermen, 1905;*
*2. & 3. Mussel fishermen*

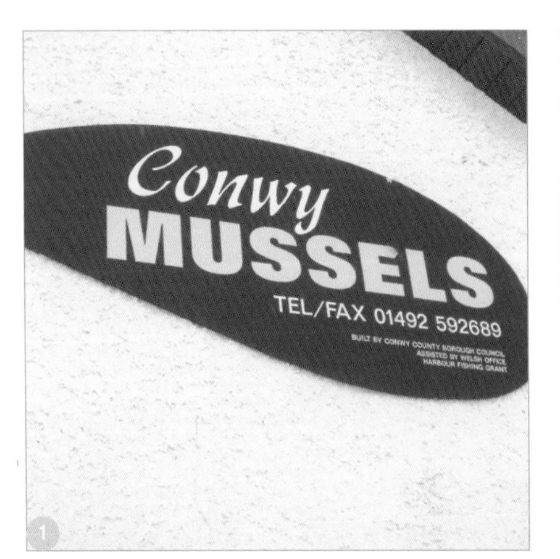
Conwy
MUSSELS
TEL/FAX 01492 592689
BUILT BY CONWY COUNTY BOROUGH COUNCIL
ASSISTED BY WELSH OFFICE
HARBOUR FISHING GRANT

fishermen had long-handled net-rakes which were used to raise the harvest until the returning tide drove them away. The shells were then carried in sacks and baskets to Cefnfro on Morfa Conwy where they were boiled in iron pots and prepared for market.

Gathering mussels as seafood became more profitable eventually – the tradition methods remained the same: handpicking in the shallows and raking the deeper pools. The Ministry of Agriculture and Fisheries stepped in with its regulations eventually and purification tanks were installed at the mouth of Afon Gyffin, upstream of the castle. Modern equipment are now used and the Conwy mussel is as tasty as ever and can be bought from the fish stall at the quay.

*1. – 3. At the Conwy Mussels museum*
*4. Mussel sculpture on the quay;*

# Sailors, Shipwrecks and Smugglers

Llandudno has a long maritime tradition. Lacking a harbour, Llandudno's characteristic craft were *flats*, or boats constructed with flat bottoms that could be sailed up onto the beach and loaded and unloaded at low tide. For centuries Llandudno remained more or less self-sufficient but as mining developed the commercial fleet increased to fifteen flats of up to 90 tons draft, all owned and operated by local people.

Llandudno's fishermen dredged for oysters in winter and spring and in the autumn caught herring. To help navigate their way along the coast, each year they travelled to Abergele to whitewash the church tower to increase its visibility from the sea. Strangely only one ship was ever constructed in Llandudno and that was a mistake. The 34-ton sloop *Sarah Lloyd* was built at Penmorfa (West Shore) and launched in 1863, just as the mines were closing down. Instead of plying a lucrative trade carrying copper ore to Swansea she was forced to eke out a precarious living tramping the coast until she was wrecked off Aberdaron in 1874.

Many ships foundered in the seas around Llandudno. In 1824 the *Hornby* was en route from Liverpool to Rio de Janeiro when it was blown onto the westernmost tip of Great Orme by a fierce gale. A sailor, named John Williams, climbed aloft to loose the jib but as the ship began to sink he leapt ashore onto a rock. Spending the night in a crevice in the rock face, now known as the Hornby Cave, in the morning he scaled the cliff to be greeted by a group of astonished miners.

The community regarded cargo washed ashore as the Lord's bounty, the harvest of the sea, but the authorities disagreed and in 1824 jailed ten Llandudno folk for 'harvesting' the wreck of the *Hornby*. When the *Archiduco Palatino* was driven onto rocks in 1847, so many people plundered the wreck that it resulted in 'The Big Excommunication'. The religious

*1. Llandudno lights from the Great Orme; 2. The old village on the Orme; 3. Orme cottage scene at Llandudno Museum*

garth ac ym maeau Llandudno a Chonwy gerllaw.
Lerpwl yn borthladd rhyngwladol prysur, roedd
ar y darn agored hwn o arfordir Gogledd Cymru.
The Great Orme and the nearby bays of
end of the 19th century when Liverpool
ships ashore on this unprotected north
Ogof Hornby
llong a ddrylliwyd
wl ar ei ffordd i
oedd cryfion
ng a suddo.
hen blaen
laflu'n glir.
garth ac yn
ymwelwyr.
Hornby Cave
SHIPWRECK!

authorities expelled every single member of Llandudno's Wesleyan Methodists, all but two Presbyterians and all but three Baptists for their role in 'Harvesting God's Bounty'!

Smuggling was another Llandudno tradition. In 1761 two Customs Officers discovered a large crowd using two small boats and a horse and cart to unload and carry away contraband from a sailing wherry. The smugglers escaped but the officers recovered several chests of tea. It was an age when even the parson enjoyed illicit duty-free refreshments.

Llandudno's maritime tradition continues. Boats take trippers around the bay for pleasure, fishing and birdwatching; there's a marina for enthusiasts at Deganwy, a sailing club on the North Shore and a boating pond for aspiring yachtsmen on the West Shore. The lives of sailors around the coast are safeguarded by Llandudno's lifeboat, which after almost 150 years valiant service has earned the town's deepest admiration and respect.

*1. Hazardous waters around the Great Orme; 2. Shipwrecks display at the Orme Visitor Centre; 3. The view from the Little Orme*

# No Place for Common People

Two hundred years ago Llandudno was a quiet, Welsh-speaking village of miners, fishermen and farmers. Most villagers combined all three activities and lived the sort of life known in Scotland as crofting. Their small houses were scattered along the lower slopes of Great Orme with twenty or so cottages lining the beach, now occupied by Llandudno's most elegant hotels.

Most of the land was owned by the Mostyn family, who lived just outside Llandudno at Gloddaeth Hall. The villagers were able to grow a few vegetables and keep a cow or a few sheep because of ancient rights under old Welsh law. One right decreed that their sheep could graze on almost 1,000 acres of common land that was unenclosed and available for all local residents to make use of. If someone had no home of their own, another right permitted them to erect a house overnight, '*tŷ unnos*', on the common and to enclose a modest amount of surrounding land to use as a garden.

Some of the old village houses can still be seen along Cwlach Street. Thomas Rowlands, an ex-copper miner, recorded tales of village life in his classic book, *Atgofion Hen Llandudno*. We learn of Tom Parry's ready wit and Owen Jones the pig-killer's stories of ghost and goblins. Apparently at Catrin's confectionery shop her animal-shaped biscuits were so ill-formed that, 'It was too great a task for any philosopher to differentiate between the dog and the ass and between the pig and the ox.' On 22 September, everyone for miles around assembled on Great Orme, to enjoy the annual Llandudno Sheep Fair at the foot of Pendinas. There was much sheep-trading but even more drinking, making friends, story-telling, fighting, poetry and just enjoying the feeling of being part of a tightly-knit community.

On 25 April 1848 Llandudno's age-old way of life came to an end. The ordinary people's common land was taken from them by an audacious act of legalised

*1. Goats on the Orme;*
*2. Disputed land*

1

2

robbery and given to the rich landowners of the parish. The total allotment acquired by the Honourable Edward Mostyn Lloyd Mostyn M.P. was 832 acres. In contrast, the common people of Llandudno were left to share a mere 1½ acres for recreation and 30 square yards for a well!

The ancient sheep fair ceased immediately, with no access to grazing land villagers could no longer keep livestock but worse was to follow. All those who relied on Welsh rights for their housing were reminded by Mostyn that a '*tŷ unnos*' had no validity in English law. Almost 100 people were evicted from their beach-side cottages, for the land was now owned by the Mostyns. Edward Mostyn hadn't yet decided whether his newly acquired beach-front development would comprise a ferry port called St George's Harbour, a dock dedicated to the export of Flintshire coal called Port Wrexham or possibly an elegant bathing resort retaining the original name.

*The Orme is still farmed today*

# By Coach, by Ferry

In the eighteenth century, any stranger travelling from Chester to Bangor needed a guide to help him reach the Conwy estuary, cross it safely and then negotiate the tidal perils and precipitous narrow paths. Even guides and ferrymen lost their lives.

Individual travellers and the mailcoach started to use the northern coastal road. The Conwy Races attracted huge crowds to the Morfa until 1794 and Conwy fairs were renowned far and wide. Hyde Hall wrote of the display of fruit offered for sale – peaches, nectarines and grapes were grown within the walls which possessed 'a flavour and a richness superior' to any found elsewhere.

Conwy hostelries, however, had a bad reputation, but even early authors mention a few good inns. The King's Head (now a part of the Castle Hotel), Red Lion, Bull, Eagles, Swan and Harp are all registered before 1769. As the eighteenth century progressed, travel increased on the 'Great Irish Road', as the coastal road was called, even though the state of the roads and ferries were designed for horseback journeys. In 1753, no less than eight horse-drawn coaches left Chester for Holyhead within 48 hours. Conwy became a compulsory stop for horse-changing and waiting for the correct conditions. The larger carriages could not manage the steep climb to Sychnant and the sharp fall to Dwygyfylchi and had to tackle the sands around Penmaenbach and Penmaenmawr at ebb-tide. The tides were dangerous, the estuary was muddy and the banks hid treacherous quicksand underfoot. Coaches overturned and got bogged down.

Up to the first half of the twentieth century, half a dozen ferrymen were still operating across the narrow river mouth opposite Deganwy. There was a ferry point here since medieval times, but when the coaching days arrived the coach was carried on large, flat-bottomed ferryboats which crossed from where is now called 'Glan Conwy corner'. These were clumsy and could not always cross the estuary. Passengers had to wait for hours in the Conwy taverns for their coach to follow them.

The ferrymen were also notorious for

*An old print of the estuary ferry*

*An early print of Penmaenmawr and its treacherous headland*

overcharging. Foot passengers usually paid a penny each, but coach travellers were required to pay a shilling each. It was an unpleasant journey in every sense and alternative routes were sought for. Some saw it worthwhile to travel upriver to the old Roman fort of Caerhun, and cross by the Tal-y-cafn ferry. An inland coach road was developed from Shrewsbury to Llanrwst, which later headed through the Snowdonia mountains via Capel Curig to Bangor.

Disaster struck the Conwy ferry on Christmas Day 1806 – the ferryboat carrying the Irish Mail capsized with the loss of 13 lives. At the moment when there was real danger that Conwy was going to be by-passed, the public outcry resulted in new plans for a bridge to cross the estuary to be drawn out.

# Bridging Conwy Waters

The Act of Union of Ireland and England in 1801 brought influencial travellers to tackle the journey from Holyhead and London. The question of crossing the Conwy estuary became an international matter, and a bridge was called for.

Conwy had been built so that the river was a natural barrier to the town. The time had come to make the town more accessible and the colonialisation of Ireland this time gave Conwy a new breath of life.

Thomas Telford was already engineering two roads across northern Wales – the A5 from Shrewsbury through the mountains to Bangor and the A55 from Chester, following the coast to Bangor. The original concept was an arched bridge, connected from a rocky island opposite Conwy castle to the eastern side by an embankment. This cob, a third of a mile long, was created with picks and shovels in an intense battle against the river and sea

*The Telford tollgate and the Conwy Suspension Bridge*

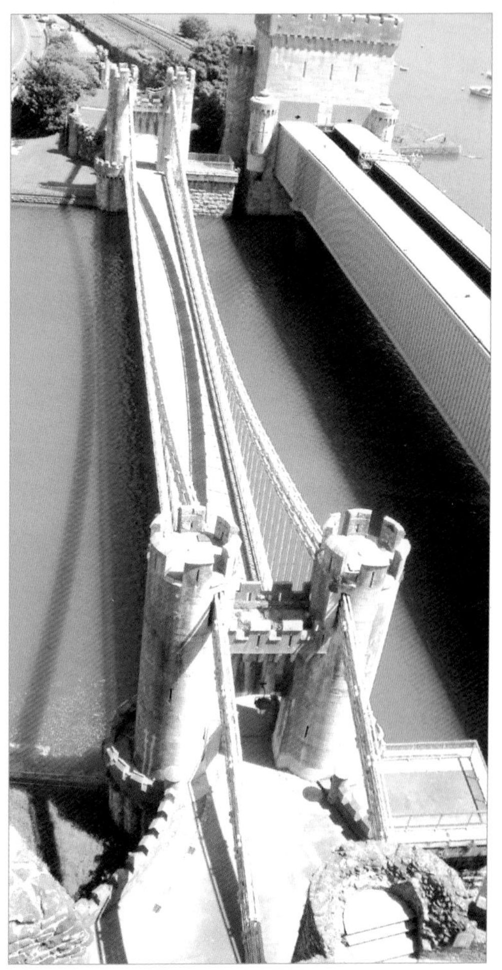

The Smallest House
IN GREAT BRITAIN
YSBWRIEL
LITTER

currents. This was revised when Telford started on the Menai Suspension Bridge in 1819. Telford's Conwy Suspension Bridge was completed in 1826, after taking four years to build. It would be the only crossing for vehicles and pedestrians for 133 years. Its span is 327 feet (98 m), its towers blend in with the castle backdrop, which also anchors the weight of the suspended deck of the bridge. A road was cut into the north-eastern side of the castle rock and a new and noble gateway was constructed to the town. The bridge is now National Trust property and the tollkeeper's house has recently been restored and furnished as it would have been in 1900.

Traffic through Conwy increased dramatically. During the nineteenth century, Conwy's fortunes took an upward leap. The population boomed from 889 to 5,240 and taverns, shops and merchants were doing a roaring trade. The great flourish is reflected in a tiny house on the quay side: in 1800, it was an 'in-fill' fisherman cottage between two terraces, only 72 inches (1.8 m) wide; by the time the terrace on one side was pulled down in 1900, it was a Victorian tourist attraction open to the many who came to enjoy the town by then buying, among other things, postcards of the 'Smallest House in Britain'.

Twenty years after Telford's suspension bridge, the iron steam engines crossed the Conwy embankment. Giant steel tubes were constructed near the Gyffin stream estuary, engineered by Robert Stephenson; stone supporting-towers were erected and six wooden pontoons were used to float the 312 feet (94 m) long massive tubes, each weighing 1,300 tons, to their lifting stations. Again the Conwy tubular railway bridge is a

lesser companion to a similar structure crossing Afon Menai, taking the railway line onwards for the Irish ferry port. The first stone was laid in 1846 and both railway lines were operational by 1849. Stephenson, like Telford, had to breach the town walls for his new route which he later bridged with an elegant skewed arch near the railway station.

*The Conwy tubular railway bridge*

# A Genteel Watering Place

Llandudno's seafront is sublime. Elegant, architecturally uniform buildings line a gently curving bay. It is without doubt Britain's finest testimony to the nineteenth century's devotion to the efficacy of immersion in seawater. In 1858 Doctor Colley settled in Llandudno and published a Medical Guide advertising the health-giving advantages of the town.

Colley recommended 15-30 minutes daily immersion in the sea and commended the warm seawater treatments available in the Llandudno Baths establishment. Erected on the site of the present Grand Hotel the Baths opened in 1855 and also offered billiards, a library, reading room and a sea-viewing balcony. In 1860 Doctor Norton of Chester opened an even more lavish Hydropathic Establishment which remains open as a hotel. In 1867 Llandudno became the first place in Wales to add a Turkish Baths to its range of therapeutic facilities.

Sea-bathing at Llandudno was a highly regulated activity, with rules on when, where and what to wear laid down by a Board of Improvement Commissioners. Naked bathing was strictly forbidden and separate sea-bathing areas delineated for males and females. When Mr D. R. Thomas was caught 'bathing within two hundred yards of the ladies' bathing ground' in 1896 he was fined a shilling (5p). Licentious bathing behaviour persisted. In 1867 Mrs Atkins of Gloddaeth Crescent claimed she was compelled to relinquish her lease because of the continued presence of nude bathing outside her seafront windows. There were repeated claims that men were removing their bathing aprons and in 1879 the Commissioners complained of men emerging from ladies' bathing machines! Standards slipped significantly in 1894 when a mixed bathing zone was permitted for those wearing the 'University or full-bathing costume'.

Several of Llandudno's bathing-machine businesses were begun by families evicted from beachside cottages who knew the tides inside out. Ex-miners

*Early postcards of the resort at Llandudno*

LIPTON

BELMONT
SAVING LIVES
AT SEA

organised informal tours of the abandoned copper mines in exchange for coins from tourists. The Welsh saying '*mae mistar ar Mistar Mostyn*' ('there is a master on Mister Mostyn') derives from these means of survival. Copper miner Thomas Kendrick became a lapidary and sold polished beach stones to visitors to provide his income. When he used his old underground skills to enlarge a cave on Great Orme for a workshop he made an historic discovery and uncovered the remains of the town's first visitors who had arrived 13,000 years earlier!

Seaside entertainment was offered by Professor Beaumont who thrilled Edwardian visitors with death-defying dives from Llandudno pier. At night he added to the excitement by entering the water enclosed in a flaming sack! Less dramatic but more enduring was Richard Codman's show. His Punch and Judy began in 1864 and continues to delight audiences under the able direction of Codman's descendants.

After 103 years Llandudno's last bathing machine finally disappeared in 1958 when proprietor, William Jones, retired. Nowadays many hotels incorporate their own lavish bathing facilities, swimming pools, massage and spa treatments, so Llandudno continues to offer visitors therapeutic relaxation.

# Celebrated Hotels and Celebrity Visitors

The first seafront hotel in Lord Mostyn's new bathing resort, the St George's, opened in August 1854. The proprietor, Isaiah Davies, had been licensee of the King's Head, a public house once much frequented by miners and today popular with residents and holidaymakers. St George's was an instant success with Llandudno's new, sophisticated clientele. Guests included Napoleon III and Empress Eugenie, Bismark, Disraeli, John Bright and Gladstone.

Soon many more hotels were erected along the seafront. The Marine Hotel was favoured by the Queen of Romania, better known under her pen name of 'Carmen Sylva'. She arranged her visit thinking Llandudno would be a quiet, restful, rural retreat and was shocked to be greeted with a rousing welcome in a lively and fashionable resort. Nevertheless, she was so touched by her reception and so enchanted by her surroundings that Llandudno left a lasting impression on her, and she, in return left an abiding impression on the town. Several streets still bear her name, the Marine Hotel displays her letter of thanks and Llandudno adopted her parting words as its official motto.

In 1861 St Tudno's Hotel was the choice of the Lidell family, which included the eponymous heroine of Lewis Carroll's internationally acclaimed novel, Alice in Wonderland. Exemplifying the high-class character of Llandudno's tourist trade Dean Lidell's party included his wife, five children, footman, lady's maid, nurse, governess and nursery maid. No wonder he thought it more convenient to have a house built to accommodate future visits to the town. Lidell's house, Penmorfa, still dominates Llandudno's West Shore and offers its guests spectacular panoramic coastal views.

Trevone Hotel was the haunt of Matthew Arnold who visited Llandudno in pursuit of his interest in Celtic literature.

*1. St George's Hotel; 2. The Queen of Romania's signature at The Marine; 3. One of the Alice themes at Llanudno; 4. The Grand Hotel*

St. GEORGE'S HOTEL
THE TERRACE
1

haven of peace!
God bless old
all its good people!
Elisabeth
2

3

GRAND HOTEL
4

erforming Birds.
Llandudno.

Attending the 1864 National Eisteddfod, Arnold was greeted by a banner which read, '*Croesaw i Deml Athrylith*' (Welcome to the Temple of Genius).

Arnold's interest in Llandudno's Celtic heritage was shared by Tracy Turnerelli, a tireless campaigner against the nineteenth-century commercialisation of Great Orme. In his, *Orme's Head Leaflet, Number One*, Turnerelli awaited with trepidation the indignities awaiting Great Orme, 'Heaven alone knows what other projects are in store to degrade, and annihilate this grand old mountain on which Druids have sacrificed, Roman armies have marched, Saints and Hermits have lived, prayed and Chieftains have held their court and sway.'

Great Orme is now formally protected and its historic and environmental importance guarded by a team of wardens. Preserving and interpreting Llandudno's unique past is widely recognised as the key to future commercial success. Tracy Turnerelli can rest in peace.

*Seaside entertainment at Llandudno – past and present*

# Trains, Trams and Paddle Steamers

The nicest way to arrive in Llandudno is to step onto the pier from one of the ships that occasionally bring visitors from Liverpool and the Isle of Man. Not so long ago thousands of trippers arrived daily aboard paddle steamers like the *St Tudno*, the *St Elian* and the lamented *La Marguerite*. Nowadays these occasional, nostalgic boat trips are eagerly anticipated and tickets sought after by tourists and residents alike.

Older visitors often recall the trams that from 1907 to 1956 ran from Llandudno's West Shore to Colwyn Bay (and for a while as far as Old Colwyn). They've gone now but a beautiful old circular passenger shelter remains at West Shore and local enthusiasts are restoring an old tram for permanent exhibition. Part of the old track can be seen in the front garden of Llandudno Museum.

Still operating, having celebrated its centenary in 2003, the unique tramway that climbs to the summit of Great Orme, is a much-loved feature of Llandudno. Its picturesque carriages are hauled up the steep slopes of the mountain by an underground cable system powered originally by a steam engine but now by electric motor. Passengers are rewarded with magnificent views as the tram ascends Great Orme and although the tramway was conceived as primarily a tourist attraction, before the age of cars and lorries it also performed an essential service for the local community. Llandudno Council required the tram company to, 'make provision for the conveyance at a reasonable and fixed charge and in a decent and seemly manner of corpses for internment in St Tudno cemetery'.

The railway reached Llandudno in 1859 but at first travel along the branch line from Llandudno Junction was far from comfortable. Because of an insufficiency of railway engines the carriages were often pulled along the line by horses and when the wind blew in the wrong direction passengers were sometimes asked to get out and push! Nowadays the service is more reliable although not quite up to the

4
St. TUDNO
GREAT ORME TRAMWAY

4
St. TUDNO
GREAT ORME TRAMWAY

standard provided by the luxurious pre-war Club Trains that daily conveyed businessmen commuting to their offices in Manchester from their homes in Llandudno.

Modern trains offer a fast, reliable service to Manchester and connections to stations beyond, but to enjoy exquisite scenery at its best you should opt for another route out of Llandudno. The Conwy Valley line is one of Wales' best-kept secrets, in just over an hour passengers travel from seaside Llandudno to Blaenau Ffestiniog in the heart of Snowdonia. Climbing aboard at Llandudno, after passing Deganwy marina, passengers catch sight of Conwy castle before reaching the lush grazing meadows of the lower Conwy valley. Travelling along the valley, the views across the river to the peaks of the Carneddau are dramatic and ever-changing. Presently passengers pass the dark forests surrounding Betws-y-coed and ascend the rocky uplands before plunging into the total darkness of a long tunnel and finally emerging into the lunar-like, slate strewn landscape of Blaenau Ffestiniog.

# Morfa Conwy

Conwy is fronted by the river and backed by the mountains. To the north-east is a wooded knoll, with low-lying grassland and dunes beyond. This area of sand, sea and marsh, the Morfa, was part of Edward I's grant of land to the thirteenth century Borough. Over the years the Morfa has been exploited for a variety of civil and military purposes whilst the hilly land on its south-eastern fringe was developed as a park and mansion in the eighteenth century. The area provides stunning river, estuary and marine views.

Conwy Morfa has provided useful grazing land for the town since at least the foundation of Aberconwy abbey in the twelfth century. Every burgess with a house or land in Conwy was permitted to graze animals on the Morfa, but had to pay the Town Corporation for the privilege. A Marsh Warden, or Keeper, was appointed and attempts at unwarranted intrusion were swiftly dealt with. In the seventeenth century typical charges were four shillings for a horse and two shillings each for cattle, for three months grazing.

The Morfa was also the venue for the annual Conwy Race Meeting and it is now the site of the Conwy United Football Club ground. Football has officially been played on the Morfa since at least 1894 when Conwy originally applied to join the new North Wales Coast Football Association. In 1903 the club was in trouble when the referee of their match against Porthmadog complained that he had been 'under threat from the Conwy crowd of 200 to 300 supporters'!

The Morfa also hosts probably Wales' first golf course. The 10 April 1903 issue of *Golf Illustrated* claimed that: 'It is well authenticated that in 1869 three enthusiastic gentlemen hailing from Scotland laid out a nine-hole golf course on Conwy Morfa'. In 1876 Jack Morris, the club professional of the Royal Liverpool improved the course on behalf of a group of members who regularly holidayed in Conwy. Unfortunately both parties neglected to find a separate club organisation to administer this new course. By the time that local players

*The Morfa at Conwy and an early camp on the site*

eventually got around to doing this in 1890 they had been pipped at the post by both Tenby (founded, November 1888) and Rhyl (March 1890). The founding meeting of the Caernarfonshire Golf Club eventually took place in Conwy Guildhall on 30 June 1890. The club and its Morfa course swiftly secured a good reputation, and in 1899 hosted the Welsh Amateur Golf Championships. The Welsh Professional Championship followed in 1905. Over the years the club has seen its course and its clubhouses fall victim to the adverse effects of fire, the army and the Expressway, but has adapted and survived to celebrate its centenary.

(extracts from *Walks from Conwy*, Christopher Draper)

*The golf course and the marina at Morfa Conwy*

# The Tunnel and the Marina

Better lines of communication had an effect on the future development of the northern Wales coast. It soon became fashionable to trip to the seaside from the industrial towns and cities. Lancashire and Deeside factory workers soon flocked to Welsh beaches and spas for health and leisure reasons. With the railroad, Llandudno sprang into existence overnight in 1850s and was a major resort by the 1880s. Colwyn Bay developed in 1890s. For a while, Conwy and the immediate area were served well by the railroad network.

In the 1920s and 30s, however, the sudden increase in the use of motor vehicles had a dramatic effect on the narrow streets of the town centre. The toll on the suspension bridge created lengthy queues and there were plans for a motor route that would have destroyed Conwy's quay. Eventually a new road bridge opened in 1958, sweeping the traffic problem right through the centre of the town, creating even more congestion and making the old streets miserable for everybody.

The planners went to work again and in the interest of heritage and conservation the Conwy estuary tunnel was finally accepted as inevitable, Conwy was to be freed of its 5 mile (8 km) tailbacks every holiday weekend as the northern coast road – now upgraded to a double carriageway and recognised as a major European international link – would by-pass one of the finest examples of medieval-walled towns.

The estuary was on the world engineering map once again as the first immersed tube tunnel was built and lowered into the river bed. Six reinforced concrete units were fabricated on the Morfa – a site which had forty years previously seen the large-scale building of Mulberry Harbours for the Normandy landings of the Second World War. The excavated basin was on the Morfa side of the estuary – this was eventually flooded and the concrete sections were floated

*1. The 1958 road bridge at Conwy;*
*2. Constructing the Mulberry Harbours*

precisely into place in a deep trench that had been dredged in the river bed. In May 199, a great sponsored walk marked the opening of a tunnel which was as remarkable an historic engineering feat as any that the shores of Conwy had seen over the ages.

A by-product of the floating sections was a flooded basin on Morfa Conwy. The estuary had long harboured pleasure boats and sailing yachts, side by side with the working fishing fleet of Conwy. Now the leisure boats would have their own moorings in a new purpose-built marina on the Morfa. This was further developed to include accommodation, shops and an inn.

On the other side of the old Conwy embankment, the mud flats on the eastern bank had been filled in with the large amount of spoil that came out of the trench in the river bed. This was reclaimed and landscaped as a reed-fringed lagoon and an RSPB reserve was established here in 1993. It matured and attracted birds rapidly. It now has a visitor centre, picnic area, birdwatching hides, nature trails and a wealth of wildlife under the dramatic scenery of Snowdonia and the Conwy estuary.

*The tunnel, the marina and the golf course*

# A Resort for All Seasons

Snowdonia is kind to Llandudno, it provides a stunning visual backdrop and an effective umbrella. Sheltered by the mountains the area enjoys a climate almost as sunny and dry as the south of England, but with milder winters and more dramatic scenery. The appeal of the climate is complemented by the wide variety of Llandudno's attractions.

Happy Valley is a beautiful public garden overlooking the sea and an ideal place for relaxation. Golf enthusiasts are spoilt for choice with three clubs, The North Wales, Maes-du and Rhos-on-Sea on the edge of town. The old course on Great Orme, developed in conjunction with the mountain tramway, has long since disappeared but three interesting innovations have taken its place. The cable lift from Happy Valley offers the longest ride in Britain and the best views in northern Wales. More challenging is the artificial ski slope, opened in 1987, which stands alongside a breathtaking toboggan run. If you've any energy left visit the sports area off Builder Street West for a spot of snakeboarding, skateboarding, rollerblading or BMX Freestyle.

Others interested in heritage might prefer Francis Chardon's fascinating house of curiosities, otherwise known as Llandudno Museum. Chardon was the Indian-born son of wealthy indigo planters who travelled the world as an artist and collector. When he died in Llandudno he bequeathed his house, pictures and antique collection to the town. Oriel Mostyn, in Vaughan Street regularly exhibits challenging artwork whilst The Alice in Wonderland Centre and The World-War-Two Homefront Experience attract visitors with their more traditional displays.

Llandudno offers no end of interesting refreshment places. In 1907 Llandudno's Cocoa House was the choice of women who founded Wales' first Female Suffrage Society on the premises. Sir Thomas Lipton's 1887 Haulfre holiday home would suit those preferring a country cottage style café who might be interested to learn that the surrounding gardens were opened

34

Pebble
Pebble Fish & Chips
PEBBLE
FOOD

to the public by Lloyd George. The beautiful Palladium building in Gloddaeth Street offers meals and alcoholic beverages and an opportunity to view one of Llandudno's most stunning interiors. From 1920-2000 the Palladium served as a cinema and theatre and details of its entertaining history can be read from its attractive wall-displays.

Wales is famous for its male-voice choirs and the best of these can be seen and heard at performances hosted by St John's and other chapels in the town centre. Llandudno's summer festival of arts and music is the cultural highlight of the year. Occasionally incorporating a visit by the Welsh National Opera to Llandudno's North Wales Theatre, the festival offers a wide variety of other activities including talks and walks exploring the history of the town.

Llandudno's Victorian Extravaganza and Transport Festival takes place every May. The town comes alive with the sounds and smells of an old-fashioned steam-powered funfair, Bodafon Fields plays host to hundreds of antique vehicles which process through the streets to the delight of the assembled crowds, many of whom attend in period costume. Whatever the time of year Llandudno is a fascinating place, a resort for all seasons.

## Walking with History

The Marine Walk downstream from Conwy quay runs along the water's edge, bordering on the old pleasure gardens of a mansion (Bodlondeb) built by a member of a local prominent family in 1742. The quay itself has many attractions to locals and visitors, including fresh catches by the fishermen.

The life in the town goes on. The Welsh, categorised as 'foreigners' and excluded when the town was founded, have long made it their own. The typical terrace cottages and high chapels have stamped their style on the old fortress colony and its culture became one with that of the surrounding valleys. When John Wesley visited the town in 1754, he met whole families that were monolingual speakers – their whole lives were lived through the Welsh language. Conwy natives, born within the town walls, are familiarly known as 'jackdaws' by the valley people.

In 1851, a national three-day eisteddfod was held inside Conwy castle. Poets, harpists, vocalists submerged the town in a festival of music and literature and the atmosphere was surely similar to that of Maelgwn's old competition on Mynydd y Dref, a millennium earlier. Special railway trains brought masses of followers from all over Wales to the town and the town's arms adorned the castle walls, proudly carrying the motto: '*Oes y byd i'r iaith Gymraeg*' (Long live the Welsh language).

Welsh food and Welsh crafts today bring a new kind of commercialism to the town that has recently benefited from re-paving road surfaces in the wake of solving its traffic problems – it has kept its integrity as a market town, offering the best of its culture without selling its soul in pieces of souvenirs. It displays its medieval grandeur with pride, proud also that its Welsh culture has survived the military attempt at its extinction. Visitors flock to its walls, its quay, its castle and its streets from every part of Europe and America, admiring it as a World Heritage Site, enjoying its atmosphere and its ability to absorb other cultures without losing its own. It is still very much a lived in town,

*1. Conwy castle and quay; 2. Bodlondeb; 3. A heritage sign*

Tŵr Llewelyn
Llewelyn's Tower

CARMEL

ST. DAVIDS DAY
1845
COMMENCEMENT OF THE
CHESTER AND HOLYHEAD
RAILWAY
CONWY TUNNEL
ENGINEER - ROBERT STEPHENSON
ERECTED BY CONWY TOWN COUNCIL

not a walled open-air museum (information: *www.conwy.gov.uk*). Business is as usual; the marina may be for pleasure but Conwy quay is still a working fishing port.

Upriver, Bodnant Gardens, now in the care of the National Trust, is a major attraction and was established in 1875 on a south-facing hill above the Conwy river, near Eglwysbach. It is a world-famous garden, noted for its botanical collections and panoramic views of the valley and the Carneddau mountains. Created by five generations of one family, this 32-hectare (80-acre) garden is superbly located with plants from all over the world. With expansive lawns and intimate corners, grand ponds and impressive terraces, a steep wooded valley and stream, as well as awe-inspiring plant collections, there are continually changing glorious displays of colour.

Nearby, the Bodnant Welsh Food Centre is located at Furnace Farm, in the stunning surroundings of the Conwy valley. Originally built in the eighteenth century, the buildings have been lovingly restored to provide an excellent venue for a farm shop, tea room, restaurant, cookery school and farmhouse accommodation. It also houses a National Beekeeping Centre for Wales, a bakery, a cheese factory and ice-cream dairy.

From parapet walks to river cruises, from pony trekking on Mynydd y Dref to meandering through the narrow streets of the town centre, Conwy still offers more than another outing on another holiday. Memory is embodied in the masonry; stories meet you on the streets. Its past has certainly seen turmoil and oppression, but the present has been able to find and display its own pride in its original roots, accepting the empty shell of Edward I's military garrison as a tribute to native resolve and endurance.

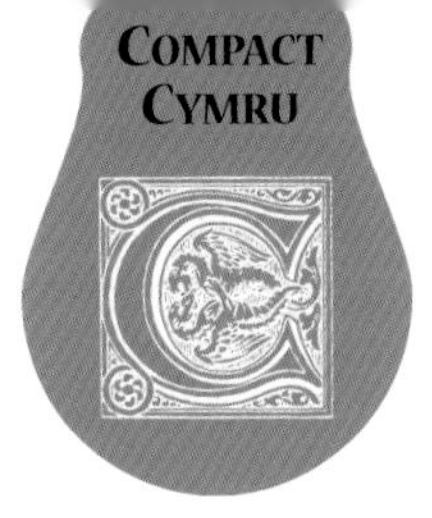


**COMPACT CYMRU**
**– MORE TITLES;**

**FULL OF COLOUR IMAGES AND CONCISE WRITING**

**www.carreg-gwalch.cymru**

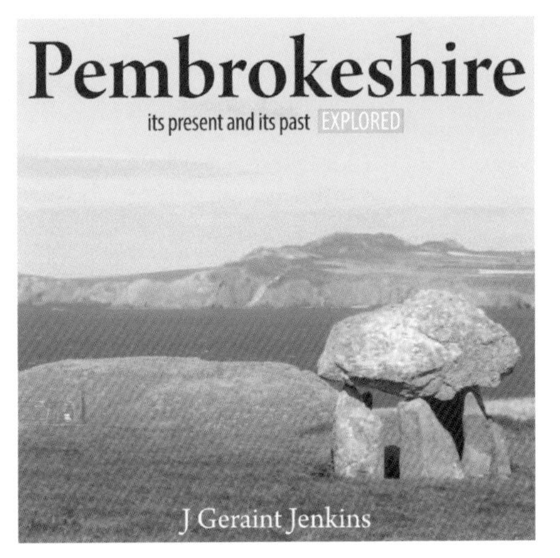


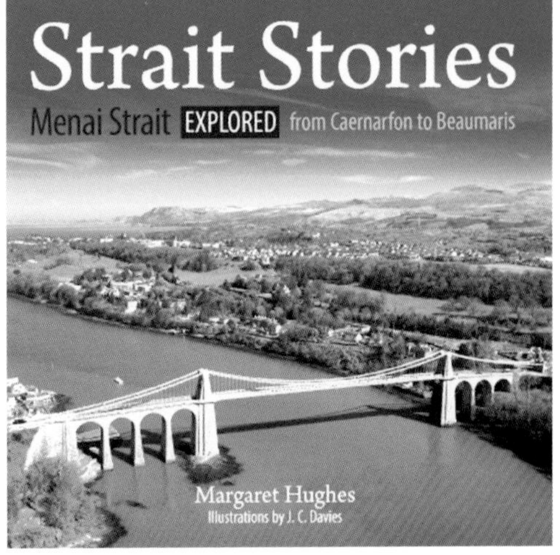

Welsh
Pub Names
TŶ COCH INN

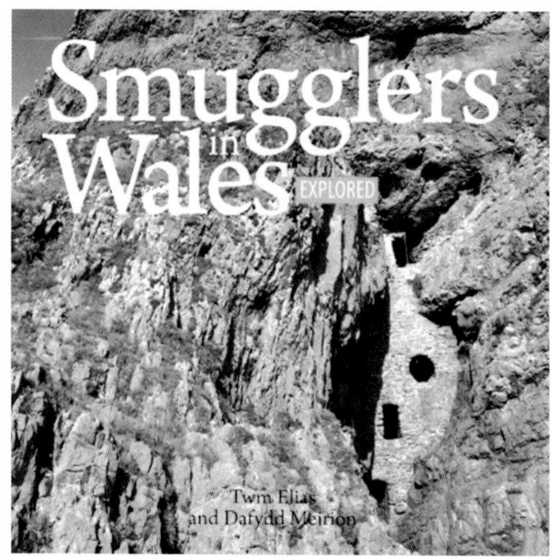
Smugglers in Wales
EXPLORED
Twm Elias
and Dafydd Meirion

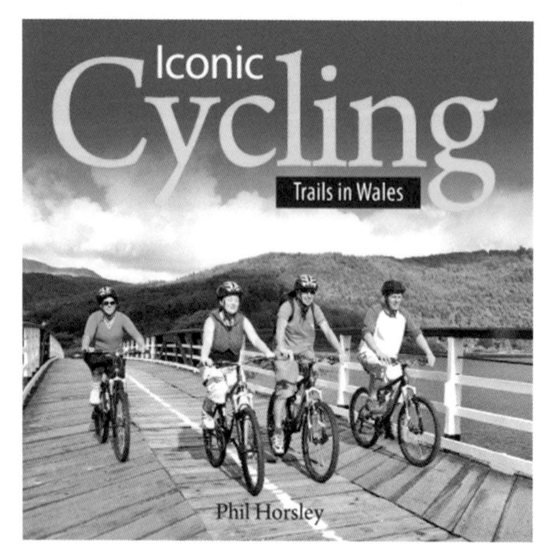
Iconic
Cycling
Trails in Wales
Phil Horsley

Battles FOR Wales
1136
Myrddin ap Dafydd

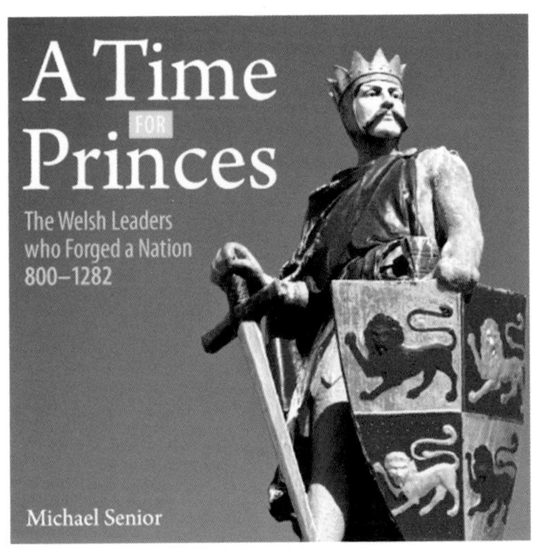
A Time
FOR
Princes
The Welsh Leaders
who Forged a Nation
800–1282
Michael Senior

The
Shepherd
War Poet
Hedd Wyn
(Ellis H. Evans 1887-1917)
introduction by Gruffudd Antur

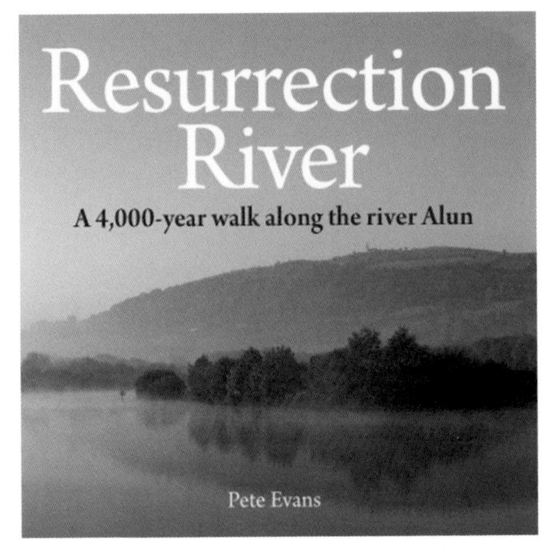
Resurrection
River
A 4,000-year walk along the river Alun
Pete Evans

Welsh Poetry
in translation
Howard Huws

Jean Napier
Rhinogydd
Ancient Routes and Old Roads

Snowdon
and its
Villages
EXPLORED

The
Great Trains
of Wales
EXPLORED
Arfon Haines Davies

Welsh
Place Names
EXPLAINED

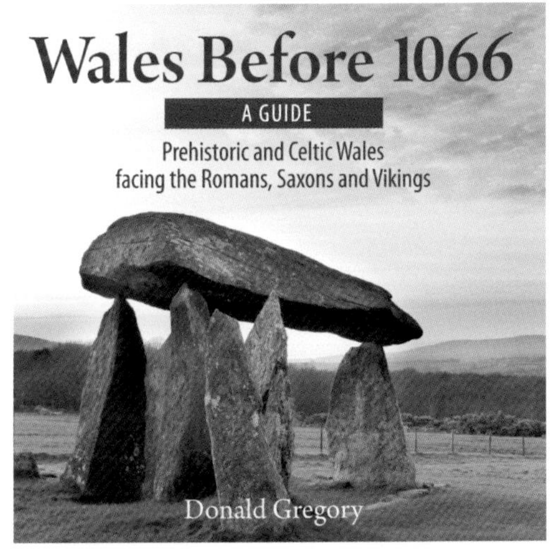
Wales Before 1066
A GUIDE
Prehistoric and Celtic Wales
facing the Romans, Saxons and Vikings
Donald Gregory

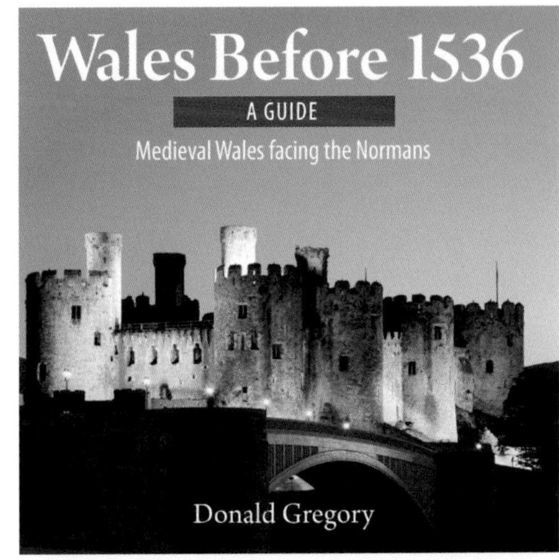
Wales Before 1536
A GUIDE
Medieval Wales facing the Normans
Donald Gregory

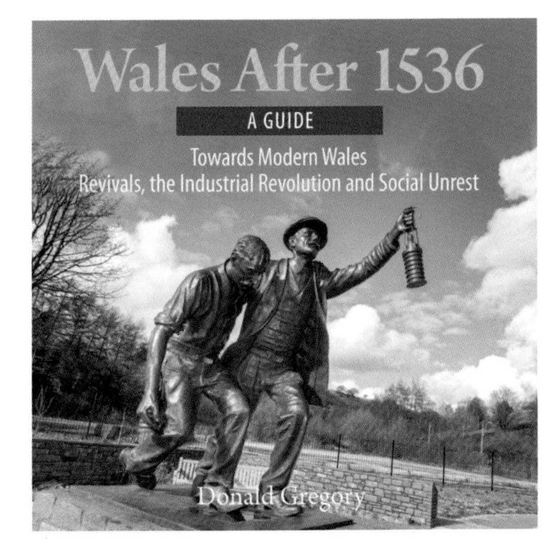
Wales After 1536
A GUIDE
Towards Modern Wales
Revivals, the Industrial Revolution and Social Unrest
Donald Gregory

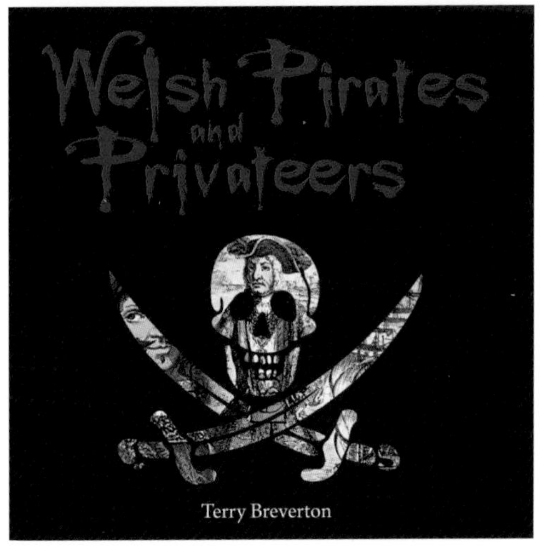
Welsh Pirates and Privateers
Terry Breverton